Improvement Leadershi

CW00471057

SELECTING GREAT IMPF
PROJECTS

How to identify and select business improvement and Lean Six Sigma projects that deliver real and quantifiable value.

Revised August 2020

While project selection is only *one* of the elements in succeeding with with business improvement, it's a vitally important element. And it is actually the role of line managers to do this as part of their work in delivering business plans and continually improving their business.

by George Lee Sye

MAIN TOPICS

Basic opportunity identification - Value stream method - The waste reduction approach - Business driver analysis - Constraint analysis - Customer related performance - Top down or bottom up identification - Prioritising projects - Selling and managing projects

SOARENT PUBLISHING
PO Box 267, Ravenshoe, Qld, AUSTRALIA, 4888

Other books by the author - https://georgeleesye.com/

Table of Contents

Introduction

Lean Six Sigma is really a business improvement strategy. And let's face it, *most* companies are doing business improvement in one form or another.

A question that I frequently get asked by executives wanting to pursue Lean Six Sigma in their business is this:

> *'How do I convince the other executives that we should be doing Lean Six Sigma when they believe we are already doing business improvement?'*

As we develop the answer to this question, the clues will emerge as to why this book is so important.

Solution Focused

Let's first be clear on *what* business improvement is for most organisations. What I've found over the past decade is that *most* organisations have a similar approach to business improvement.

Let's take a simple example to explain what I mean. The following comprises a list of business improvement initiatives for a medium sized clothing manufacturing business.

BUSINESS IMPROVEMENT PROJECTS

Expand the warehouse and implement a bar coding system

Renegotiate 'per unit' supply rates from the suppliers of blank shirts

Implement a 'cascading' based system of performance management

Negotiate a new freight contract

Introduce the PASS safety system across all warehouses

Replace key access with proximity card system

Distribute a quarterly company newsletter

Individually cling wrap dress shirts

Negotiate a corporate alliance with the Zenith Hotel chain

What do you make of that list?

Notice this one thing; that the list of initiatives is simply a list of *solutions*. Look at it ... each idea is a way of *solving* some perceived problem. For example, renegotiation of unit supply rates is simply a solution for the problem of increasing costs to produce a unit of whatever they make.

In the absence of an improvement strategy like Lean Six Sigma, *this* tends to be the way business improvement is approached.

Ideas for making the business better are generated, consolidated and undertaken as improvement projects. Managers *genuinely* believe they are doing business improvement and have no idea why you would want to add a Lean Six Sigma methodology to it.

I've even seen the situation where a manager even believed the company was already doing Lean Six Sigma.

Business Improvement Ideas

```
┌─────────────────────────────┐
│                             │
│      SOLUTION KNOWN         │
│                             │
└─────────────────────────────┘
```

Common Approach to Business Improvement

Asking A New Question

So what's missing?

The major shortfall with this approach is that *many* opportunities for genuine performance enhancement are missed because solutions are not known. The approach above produces a list of ideas that are the answer to one question:

'What can we DO to improve our business?'

A company's approach to business improvement is *significantly* broadened when improvement ideas are captured for which solutions are *not* known. A new question is asked this time;

'WHERE can we improve that would add value to the business?'

In the case of our clothing manufacturer for example, answers to this question might generate ideas like these.

- The number of incidents of incorrect order processing

- The cycle time for turning around an order

- The proportion of on-time creditor payments

Any of these are worthwhile projects to undertake because they positively impact customers and the business itself. Yet none of these is a solution, only a focal point for improvement.

Business Improvement Ideas

SOLUTION **NOT** KNOWN	SOLUTION KNOWN

Broadening the Approach to Business Improvement

The Role Of Lean Six Sigma

Where methodologies such as Lean Six Sigma come into play for your organisation is in the process of identifying *solutions* for improving the performance of *processes*.

Because of the orientation of these methodologies towards the use of data, the more appropriate processes for Lean Six Sigma focus are those that are *highly cyclic* and have *repetitive* or *standardised* process steps.

For example, reducing order errors [in an order filling process] or reducing cycle time for order processing [in an order filling process] are perfect as Lean Six Sigma projects. Solutions are not known, the process is highly cyclic and steps are repetitive.

Non Lean Six Sigma Fit

Not all improvement ideas *without* solutions will be Lean Six Sigma projects.

They will however benefit from the use of Lean and Six Sigma tools in identifying and choosing solutions. For example, reducing the number of late creditor payments may be solved by using many of the facilitation and solution identification tools from the suite of Lean Six Sigma tools. However, if the team identified 'compliance with terms of payment' as the main issue, the project is obviously not a perfect fit for the Lean Six Sigma methodologies.

Opportunities such as 'improve employee morale' or 'improve staff awareness of company performance' or 'increase the quality of induction training for new employees' are also poor fits with Lean Six Sigma in its pure form. However, work on those problems will benefit from the use of Lean Six Sigma tools and processes in finding solutions.

Business Improvement Ideas		
Lean Six Sigma	Non Lean Six Sigma	
SOLUTION **NOT** KNOWN	SOLUTION **NOT** KNOWN	SOLUTION KNOWN

Business Improvement with Lean Six Sigma

The point I've been making is that business improvement *with* Lean Six Sigma is still just business improvement. However, it establishes a framework where the company works on projects where solutions are known *and* projects where solutions have yet to be identified.

And there are great advantages of having this approach in your business.

1. A PROACTIVE APPROACH to improvement of core business process performance can be undertaken. The company might *already* be meeting certain performance levels, however *new* levels can be targeted with projects intended to find out how those new levels can be reached.

2. GREATER USE OF DATA to choose improvement solutions. A genuine shift away from solving problems based on gut feel and past experience.

3. HIGHER LEVELS OF PERFORMANCE can be achieved as a vast array of the latest improvement tools and processes are introduced into the business via the Lean Six Sigma toolkit.

4. The existing business improvement system is not eliminated; no ... it is COMPLIMENTED AND ENHANCED by the *inclusion* of Lean Six Sigma. Much higher levels of commitment to the initiative may be observed by those involved in business improvement already.

That's how I go about answering the question of why a company must do some sort of Lean Six Sigma activity as a *part* of business improvement.

Okay, enough about the strategy of business improvement, that's not why we're here. Let's begin to get to the core subject of this book - improvement project identification.

Keeping It Simple

The process described in this book is just one approach, albeit a fairly robust and generic one that is suitable for companies that utilise a range of business improvement methodologies (i.e.: Six Sigma, Lean Manufacturing, Design for Six Sigma, QFD, Theory of Constraints etc).

If we were to take a look at it from a macro level, we would describe the process as having the following steps.

- IDENTIFYING improvement opportunities

- SCREENING the improvement opportunities

- PRIORITISING against important criteria

- ALLOCATING projects in their priority to whatever approach makes sense (Lean, Six Sigma, project management, process design etc)

Those that fit the essential criteria for Lean and / or Six Sigma are allocated accordingly to Lean Six Sigma Black Belts or Green Belts. Those that don't are allocated to other improvement or project management practitioners.

The step of identifying improvement opportunities is a critical one in this sequence as it is the one that sets the process up for either success or failure.

More Than One Way To Skin A Cat

There are many ways to go about identifying opportunities for improvement. We could simply ask the question, 'what do we need to do to improve our business?' The answers might not revolutionise your business, but then again they just might give you an edge over your competitors.

We don't want to take an approach quite so unsophisticated; we want to inject some science and strategy in the way in which we tackle the question of *where* and *how* to improve our businesses.

Some of the more scientific ways are these:

- Problem or performance gap *identification*

- Problem or performance gap *creation* through setting new objectives

- Business *driver* analysis

- Analysis of *processes* for constraints or bottlenecks

- Analysis of performance against *customer* expectations or any other key business measures

You may have already noticed, opportunities can and *should* be identified by taking a look at the business from a variety of angles. The moment you start to study these angles, you're able to more effectively respond to the voice of the customer, the voice of the process, the voice of the business and the voice of stakeholders in general.

What are these voices I'm talking about? Let me explain this way.

The Voice of the Customer

Identifying where gaps exist in meeting customer needs or expectations (including both internal and external customers).

The Voice of the Process

Identifying where opportunities exist to minimise undesirable variation and reduce waste from a process.

The Voice of the Business

Identifying where gaps exist in meeting business goals or achieving specific internal performance objectives (ideally linked to the strategy and business plans).

The Voice of Stakeholders

Identifying where improvements can be made in general that result in increased morale, greater satisfaction, enhanced safety of key stakeholders and stakeholder groups (such as employees, staff, owners etc).

Why There Isn't The One Way

Why would we list multiple ways to identify opportunities and not provide *the one way* to do this?

That's a fair question is it not?

Firstly, let's acknowledge that all businesses differ; no two are exactly the same. The way in which a business identifies opportunities for growth in value will be driven by many factors. Some of these might include:

1. The maturity of the organisation itself

2. The maturity of the organisation with respect to where it is in the implementation of their business improvement approach

3. The maturity of the industry in which the business is positioned

4. The way in which a business plans its business and operating strategies

5. Future market scenarios

6. Active market forces at any particular point in time

7. The culture of the organisation

Secondly, business and operating thinking patterns vary so greatly that *no* single approach is best.

When starting the process of identifying opportunities, those responsible must take these variables into account and choose the one that *best* suits their existing or anticipated situation.

In this book I've touched on the way in which *some* of these approaches *might* work. The intent is to provide you with choices so that you can logically choose a starting point for your Lean Six Sigma or business improvement project work.

Let me wrap up this introduction by quickly describing how I've laid out the book for you.

This Book

I've separated 'identification of improvement opportunities' from 'selection of projects' in the book for this reason. The identification process is designed to generate a list of potential opportunities for adding value to the business, without any consideration for how those opportunities will be addressed. Some opportunities will be appropriate to Lean or Six Sigma methodology, however many will not.

The selection process is used to sift and sort through these opportunities in a rigorous way to ensure projects allocated to any formal Lean Six Sigma initiative fit certain criteria. Opportunities not chosen for allocation to a Lean Six Sigma project team leader are still opportunities, but are best addressed using alternative approaches.

It's my intention that the content is easy to follow and you are able to find the piece of information you need without much fuss. I trust I've succeeded in achieving that.

Enjoy.

Chapter 1 - Basic Opportunity Identification

Just Ask

At the very basic level, you might implement an idea generating system whereby employees [from across the business] put forward improvement ideas.

The benefits of such an approach might include these:

- All employees can get involved in business improvement

- The voice of internal stakeholders has the opportunity to be heard, business improvement becomes a vehicle for people to make positive change using their ideas

- Many simple and easy to do improvements can be generated in a short period of time

There are two key challenges with this approach that you must be aware of.

1. **It is very easy to get overwhelmed with ideas:** You can end up in the situation where you have so many ideas that they are 'stockpiled' and many never get addressed. It won't take long for a Business Improvement (BI) initiative to lose credibility with the workforce if ideas are not acted upon in a reasonable time frame. This issue must be addressed before you roll out the idea generation process.

2. **Most ideas will be in the form of solutions:** My experience is that employees will generally tell you what they want to see *done*, in other words their idea for *how* to solve a specific issue. Without any other formal method for selecting projects, opportunities to massively impact key drivers of the business at the strategic level may *never* be realised.

Let's take a look at some other approaches.

Looking From Two Dimensions

When people think about improvement opportunities in a business, their thought processes are generally focused on one of two dimensions.

DIMENSION 1 - Problems or challenges they are experiencing in their day to day work or in the business.

DIMENSION 2 - Opportunities to make something even better than it is now.

Let's take a look at both dimensions.

Dimension 1 - Problems

When I say problem, I'm referring to gaps that exist between *expected* performance and *actual* performance in the context of key business measures. While I am more inclined to refer to problems as challenges, the word problem is appropriate in this context.

The nature of problems are such that they exist in four basic forms:

1. One-off problems or failures;

2. Frequent problems or failures;

3. New problems; and

4. Nagging problems.

One-off Problems or Failures

These are one-off occurrences or events where actual performance drops well below expected levels of performance. This type of event can usually be attributed to some special or unusual circumstance.

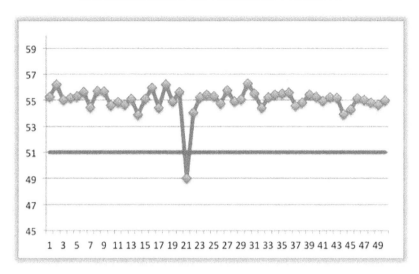

One-off Problems

Frequent Problems or Failures

These are problems that do not appear continually, but rather occur on frequent occasions as one-off events. As in the case of one-off problems, the process performs at an expected level most of the time.

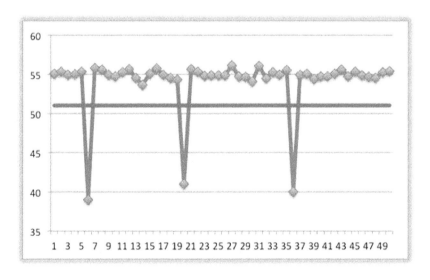

Frequent Problems or Failures

New Problems

These are problems that appear when process performance *drifts* to a level below that which was previously maintained. Something in the process has obviously changed or *shifted*.

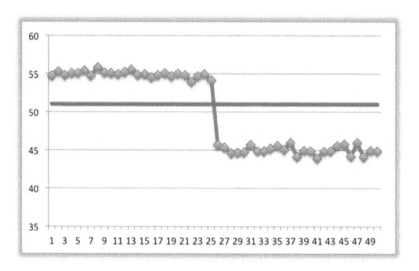

New Process Performance Problem

When *assignable* causes are identified, process performance can be raised to the level previously experienced.

Nagging Problems

These are problems that have persisted over time.

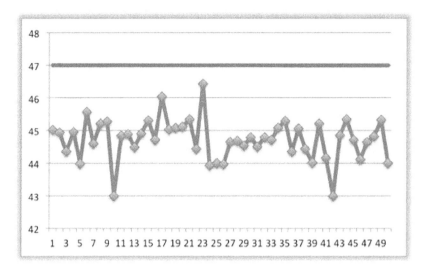

Nagging or Persistent Performance Problem

Actual performance levels have not reached expected or targeted performance levels. Two options present themselves here – *lower* the performance target or *improve* process performance.

Looking For Problems

One of the simplest ways to find these problems is to start looking for those that appear in the form of:

- Rework

- Repeating failures

- Unplanned failures

- Excess cycle time (receipt of goods, delivery, work completion, set up etc)

- Excess variation in the quality of process inputs

- Low standard or poor performance in comparison to others (yield, utilisation, usage, inventories etc)

- Not hitting targets, a gap between actual and preferred performance (recoveries, throughput volumes, yield etc)

- Customer dissatisfaction with respect to quality and / or service

- Unplanned stoppages, delays

- Excess variation in output (quality, service, delivery times, order fulfillment etc)

-Excess or unnecessary inventory or work in progress

Every single one of these is waste in a business!

The identification of these problems should occur both at the work level and at the management level.

Those responsible for the work processes are in a position to identify opportunities for improvement. A manager who asks the right questions and monitors the right measures of performance is also in a good position to identify opportunities for improvement.

Where these signs are observed, they should be discussed as potential Lean Six Sigma projects at the first opportunity.

Dimension 2 - Opportunities

It's important for all of us to remember this; problems are just challenges, they're simply opportunities to improve. Whilst an organisation does not want to live in a world of continually responding to what are perceived to be problems, where these can be addressed there may be considerable opportunity for a business.

Proactive identification of opportunities for new levels of performance can be approached in two ways.

1. Creating Problems; and

2. Reproducing High Performance.

Creating Problems

Where your perception is that you don't have any performance problems, then think about creating your own problems.

Why would I want to do that you might ask?

Like I said, problems are opportunities to improve. Smart people create problems for themselves. We can all create useful problems by specifying performance targets that produce gaps between current performance and some desired level of performance.

This simple concept is a foundation for continual business improvement. Peter Senge (1993) refers to the result of this creation of a gap as 'creative tension'. This is a tension that pulls people towards a desired outcome or desired state.

In a well managed organisation, these gaps will *always* exist as a part of the way in which improvement challenges are constantly being set at *all* levels in an organisation.

If the perception is that there are no performance gaps, it might be time to reflect on how performance is being managed.

Something worth thinking about!

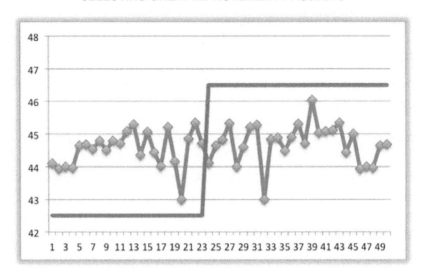

Creating Performance Gaps

A question often asked of me is this. How do you determine what those new targets should be?

New performance targets can be identified through various ways including:

Benchmarking leading companies;

Learning from subject matter experts;

Talking to customers;

Asking employees who work with the process; and

Proactively setting stretch targets as a matter of course.

Reproducing High Performance

Variation is a natural part of life, it's something we expect to see in any process. It's also possible to improve the performance of a process by studying the *higher* levels of performance within the exhibited range of variation.

The intent is to find out what it is that causes that *higher* performance and try to reproduce it consistently.

This approach uses the same methodology as trying to eliminate poor performance, albeit with a view to reproducing not eliminating.

Hopefully that makes sense. If it doesn't, this picture might help explain it.

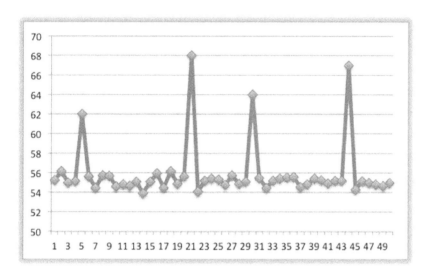

Opportunities to Reproduce Higher Performance Levels

In this case, the special higher performance events can be treated in the same way as special or one-off poor performance events. the only difference is that we want to replicate the good performance, not eliminate it.

So that's kind of the foundation information problems and opportunity identification.

Let's look at another way that we've used frequently over the past ten years.

A Simple Six Step Process

Here is a really simple, six step *facilitated* process for identifying potential projects using the problem / opportunity approach. It is designed to be undertaken with a group of company employees.

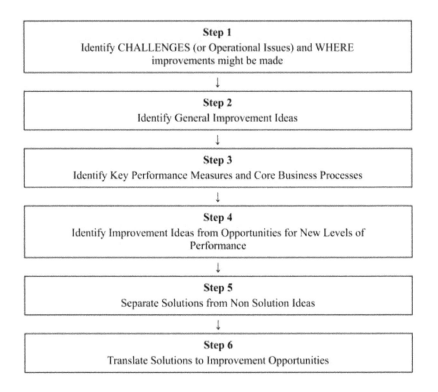

Six-Steps for Generating Business Improvement Ideas

Step 1 - Identify challenges or operational issues and .....

..... where improvement might be made.

My experience is that when *starting* the process of identifying opportunities for improvement, it is useful to engage participants in some activity that gets them thinking about the workplace. More specifically I want them to think about the **challenges and issues** they are often confronted with *and* **where** they think improvement can be made that would add value to the business.

It doesn't matter what position people hold in the organisation, *every* person feels pain when something doesn't go as well as they would like, or a nagging issue doesn't get resolved. Most people also have an opinion about where improvements can be made in an organisation, so we might as well use that.

When facilitated well, you'll probably see active discussion amongst all participants about issues close to their heart, issues they feel strongly about personally. You have them thinking about a range of issues that were not in their focus at the beginning of the session, and the transition into improvement idea generation now has some solid foundations.

The most useful questions I've found to ask here are these.

Q1. What challenges or operational issues do you deal with in your work?

Q2. Where do you think improvements can be made that would add value?

Notice we asked *where* improvements can be made, not *what* improvements can be made. A 'where' question usually prevents them coming up with a solution to the problem. We only want to know where the gap exists at this point, *not* how to solve it.

Step 2 – Identify business improvement ideas from .....

..... problems and opinions about *where* improvements can be made:

This is simply a matter of having the group brainstorm and exhaust *all* of their ideas for improvement based on their workplace challenges. My experience has been that lots of ideas are generated here, though many of them are in the form of solutions or allude to solutions.

For example, instead of saying the opportunity is to 'reduce water consumption', the idea will be a solution to that such as 'install self closing taps'. Someone might put up an idea such as 'lack of staff', which really alludes to the solution of 'increase staff'.

It's okay to leave these here at the moment, they will be addressed in the fifth step of this process.

At the end of this step you should have a broad list of ideas for improvement, and as I said, the majority will probably be solutions or lean more towards the solution side.

One thing that I've noticed is this step seems to fit better with the thinking of operational staff than it does with managers or business leaders. Bare with me for a moment if you're a manager reading this.

The real hands-on challenges are felt *more* at the operational level, so thinking about problems comes easy. The thinking of senior people tends to lean more towards higher level opportunities to grow the business.

This is the most useful question I've found to ask in this step.

Q3. What ideas do you have for improving the business based on 'challenges you have to deal with'.

Q4. What ideas do you have for improvement the business based on 'where you think improvements can be made'?

Obviously they need to be able to see their answers from Step 1 activities.

Step 3 – Identify key performance measures and .....

..... core business processes.

This work sets the group up to move away from thinking about problems, to thinking proactively about improvement.

In this step you want the group to identify the core processes they own or work in *and* what the key measures of performance are for those processes.

These measures can be business related (e.g. safety, throughput, inventory, cost per unit, utilisation etc), or they can be customer related (e.g. quality, timeliness, cycle time, non defect rates, availability etc).

By identifying and discussing key measures and the processes that are core to the business, the transition to the next step is much easier.

These are the most useful questions I've found to ask in this step.

Q5. What are your core business processes? or What processes are core to your part of the business?

Q6. What are your key performance measures for these processes? (these can include business or customer related measures)

Step 4 – Identify business improvement ideas from .....

..... opportunities for new levels of performance:

Participants discuss where they think the business can be positively impacted by targeting new levels of performance. The discussion here should flow from the work just completed in identifying core business processes *and* key performance measures.

As I said earlier, this type of thinking tends to sit well with members of the management or leadership team of a company.

What you will generate in this step will be ideas that are mostly 'non-solution' ideas. What I mean by that is the ideas will be worded like 'reduce the turnaround time to repair vehicles', without stating how that will be achieved. In other words the solution is not stated or even known.

The most useful question I've found at this step is this.

Q7. What improvements *might* we target that would positively impact performance against key measures?

The next two steps help us sort and organise our thinking around the opportunities we might work on.

Step 5 – Separate Solutions from .....

..... Non-solution Ideas:

Many of the ideas generated (particularly those from step 2) will be in the form of solutions. For example, an improvement idea like 'shutdown one line and increase the capacity of the main line' is really a solution.

'Non-solution' ideas are in the form of a statement of what needs to be improved *without* stating how it will happen. For example, 'improve the level of communication to the workforce' is not a solution because how to do it is not stated. These need to be separated because solution ideas and non-solution ideas are addressed in different ways.

The most useful question I've found is this.

Q8. Which of these ideas are solutions, which of these ideas are not solutions?

Step 6 – Translate Solutions into .....

..... Improvement Opportunities:

This is probably one of the most important steps, *and* in my experience, one of the most challenging for facilitators. I always end these sessions by having the group translate their solution ideas, or ideas that allude to solutions, into improvement opportunities.

For example, someone might put up an idea such as 'limit email forwarding to four messages per day per person'. This is clearly a solution. By asking a question such as 'what problem are you trying to solve?', you get to find out what they are trying to fix with this solution. In this case the answer might be something like this: 'we spend too much time doing email because we get so many'.

The *problem* is the foundation for you to identify a non-solution based opportunity such as 'reduce the amount of time we spend doing email'.

By doing this you get to explore many more potential solutions to solving the problem, you are not limited to one solution which might not even work.

Here's the same example in visual form.

A SOLUTION ➜	THE REAL PROBLEM ➜	IMPROVEMENT IDEA
Limit email forwarding to 4 messages per day'	Spend too much time doing email'	Reduce the amount of time we spend doing email'

From Solution to Improvement Idea

Let me give you another example.

Suppose someone presents an idea that begins with the words *lack of.* It could be something like 'lack of staff'. This idea pushes you down the path of a single solution – the obvious solution in this case is to *increase staff.*

Questions such as *how do you know you have a problem?* or *what problem are you trying to solve here?* help you get back to the *real* problem and a non-solution based improvement idea.

A SOLUTION →	THE REAL PROBLEM →	IMPROVEMENT IDEA
'Lack of Staff'	'Jobs do not get completed, excess carryover work'	'Reduce the amount of carryover work'

From 'Lack of .....' to Improvement Idea

Applying these types of questions when a solution is offered might be worth doing for a number of reasons.

First, there may not be a problem at all.

Second, there may be better ways of solving the problem than the proposed solution.

Here are the most useful questions I've found to ask in this step.

Q9. How do you know you have a problem?

Q10. What problem are you trying to solve here?

Q11. How do you know *this* is the solution to the problem?

Q12. How do you know there isn't a better way to solve the problem?

Q13. Is it possible there's a better way to solve the problem?

A Quick Summary

Business improvement idea generation from problems and performance improvement opportunities is usually the way organisations approach project selection in the early stages of their implementation of a formal Business Improvement initiative.

We could simply tackle the issue by looking at those two dimensions of problems and opportunities for improvement.

We could also expand our options and follow the six step process we described in the previous section.

While these methods will prove useful, keep in mind that as the organisation matures with its initiative, it may then shift to other ways of generating ideas. Some of these are described on the following pages.

Here Are Those Questions Again

Here are those questions again, albeit it wrapped up together in a single list.

Q1. What challenges or operational issues do you deal with in your work?

Q2. Where do you think improvements can be made that would add value?

Q3. What ideas do you have for improving the business based on 'challenges you have to deal with'.

Q4. What ideas do you have for improvement the business based on 'where you think improvements can be made'?

Q5. What are your core business processes? or What processes are core to your part of the business?

Q6. What are your key performance measures for these processes? (these can include business or customer related measures)

Q7. What improvements *might* we target that would positively impact performance against key measures?

Q8. Which of these ideas are solutions, which of these ideas are not solutions?

Q9. (for non-solutions) How do you know you have a problem?

Q10. What problem are you trying to solve here?

Q11. How do you know *this* is the solution to the problem?

Q12. How do you know there isn't a better way to solve the problem?

Q13. Is it possible there's a better way to solve the problem?

Chapter 2 - The Waste Reduction Approach

Waste Is Everywhere

Waste, by definition, sits inside every organisation and probably every organisation process.

Some of this waste will be difficult to remove. However, much of it can be removed if we see it and recognise its contribution to lower performance levels, missing business plan targets, and the way it adds unnecessary cost.

As a line manager, if you have never taken action with a view to 'waste reduction' as I will describe here, then this is one of the first and simplest things you can do to improvement your department or part of the business.

First Get Clear On What Waste Is

Let's first think about waste as:

> *(n) Anything that does not directly contribute to the process of producing a product or delivering a service to a customer.*

For example a loan application with four levels of approval contains waste. We want to clear that loan application path of waste and maximise business efficiency; this is the primary intention of Lean.

When integrated with Six Sigma, you can also generate improvements in quality and process variation, as well as improve process flow and cycle time.

To make sure we're all really clear on what waste is, we can break waste down into seven outcomes or activities. These are not my seven, they are the globally recognised way of identifying waste in organisations.

And before you run through the list, it's important to point out that even if you believe you '*must*' engage in any of these, all of them are still considered to be waste.

Here are the seven wastes:

- Defects

- Inventory

- Motion

- Transportation

- Over Production

- Waiting

- Non Value Added Processing

A useful acronym once told to me for remembering these seven forms of waste is this.

D.I.M.T.O.W.N.

DEFECTS – Any product or service that does not conform to customer specifications or expectations, and results in dissatisfaction is a defective product or service.

The hidden costs associated with defects include unnecessary labour and wasted materials. The costs that are hard to quantify are those associated with lost business in the future because of poor quality.

INVENTORY – This is waste. Goods, regardless of what they are, sitting in a store ties up capital. Hewlett Packard reported a $1 million saving in reduced inventory due to improved flow. That is cold hard cash directly in their pocket.

Inventory includes excess raw materials, work in progress, completed or finished goods as well as repair parts and supplies. Inventories not only tie up capital, they require a company to locate and allocate space and use time to handle whatever it is in the inventory.

Inventory often exists where there is a change in process ownership. It's like there is a lack of trust or low confidence issue that drives its accumulation. Non-aligned KPI's along a value chain can also impact negatively on the holding of inventory.

MOTION – This term refers to unnecessary steps or movement undertaken by workers or equipment involved in core business processes to accommodate inefficient layout or anything that does not add value to the process such as defects, reworking, reprocessing and storage.

Suppose an employee's job was to service a piece of mobile machinery, and his toolbox was in such a location that every time he needed a new tool, he had to walk five metres to the toolbox and back again. How much of the total time to service this vehicle would be involved in that movement to and from the toolbox.

Most people would say the time is of little consequence. How much time would that amount to over the course of a full year? I think you'd agree that the total accumulated time would probably be equal to the time it would take to service a number of vehicles.

The point is this, motion adds time to a process, just like transport, and is ultimately wasted time. Seen once, it seems like a nothing, but it accumulates and offers a great opportunity to increase throughput for no more effort.

TRANSPORTATION – This is unnecessary movement of materials such as the movement of partially completed units from one operation to another. Transportation results in (a) additional non value adding time to a process, and (b) increased risk of damaged units.

OVER PRODUCTION – Over production is the continued production of units resulting in excess quantities that must be stored.

In effect, over production is the creation of products before the customer actually needs them and results in the creation of inventory.

WAITING – We can also refer to waiting as queueing. In this context, waiting is a period of inactivity in a downstream process that is the result of an upstream process not delivering on time.

NON VALUE ADDED PROCESSING – This term refers to additional or extra activities such as reworking, re-handling, reprocessing and storage. These are usually the result of over production, excess inventory and defects.

We can also refer to this as 'over processing'.

T.I.M.W.O.O.D.

Those seven wastes can also be presented in a different sequence that some of our customer companies refer to by the acronym T.I.M.W.O.O.D.

- Transportation

- Inventory

- Motion

- Waiting

- Over Production

- Over Processing (aka Non Value Added Processing)

- Defects

It doesn't matter which acronym you use, as long as you recognise the waste.

The Line Manager's Waste Walk

What you can do as a manager is leave your office, and do what we refer to as a 'Waste Walk'.

You simply take the time to walk through the offices or work areas associated with your area of responsibility, and look for signs of waste.

You look for these types of signs:

- Blocked pathways that impede movement

- Excess inventory (i.e. parts, tools, consumables, physical products in stores etc)

- Products discarded because they have faults

- Piles of paperwork

- People getting in the way of each other when they work

- Stuff stored in work areas that are no longer needed or used

- Tools laying about disorganised

- Dirty and cluttered work areas

- Missing items (i.e. shadow boards, storage areas etc)

- Customers complaining about a product or service

- Long changeover cycle times where production has stopped

- Worn out and hard to see work area demarcation lines

- Old reports and irrelevant notices on notice boards

- Meetings running way over time

I could go on as the list can pretty much be as long as you want. I think you get the gist of this.

The question now is *what do you do with those observations?*

It's simple - as a line manager you discuss these with your direct reports and get to work on embedding a culture of 'waste elimination'.

You get them to see it and do something about it … and you hold them accountable. And you congratulate them and reinforce good behaviours when they take place.

Setting It Up

It's absolutely vital that you recognise your role in creating a culture of 'waste elimination' through giving this constant attention and reinforcing the behaviours you want repeated.

What obviously interests you as the manager will fascinate those who work for you. And when your direct reports are given some type of kudos for doing something positive in this area of interest, they will be more likely to repeat that behaviour.

But you should also consider teaching your direct reports about 'waste elimination' as part of setting this up.

In any company with an active business improvement initiative, you will have resources you can call upon to help out with that education process; you should use them to teach about the value of DIMWTOWN, or TIMWOOD, whatever the case may be.

Chapter 3 - Value Stream Method

Two Types Of Processes

Michael Porter (as presented by Mintzberg and Quinn - 1996) describes business processes as being of two types - Primary Processes and Secondary Processes.

Let me start this chapter with a discussion of the latter.

Secondary Processes

These are the processes involved in supporting primary processes. Through the provision of inputs, technology, human resources, and various other organisation wide functions, secondary processes support or enable the creation of value.

Secondary processes most commonly include those that are associated with:

- Supply and procurement

- Information technology

- Human resource management

- Business infrastructure

Primary Processes

By contrast, primary processes are those involved in the actual or physical creation of the products or services, their sale and transfer to customers, and after sales service.

Primary processes are those that actually create value for the business, and usually include these major elements:

- Inbound logistics

- Operations

- Outbound logistics

- Marketing and sales

- Service

The diagram below shows how the two relate to one another. Primary processes are represented across the top as the major steps that create the outputs the company passes on to customers. Secondary processes are shown supporting these from the bottom of the diagram.

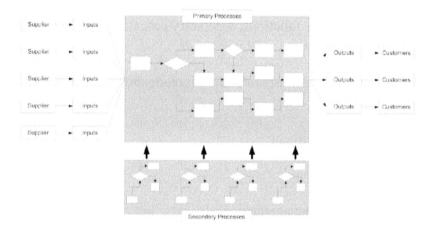

Primary and Secondary Business Processes

That's an overview of business processes. Let's explore the value stream concept.

The Idea Of A Value Stream

We might define a Value Stream in this way:

Value Stream (n): The consolidated sequence and flow of all of the activities or operations required for the design, ordering, production and delivery of products or services to a customer.

So when we talk about value streams, we are really discussing the major process components in their linear sequence from the most upstream point of design to the end point of delivery to the customer. In other words, a reference to the primary process of a business.

Single or Multiple Value Streams

Depending on the organisation, the company's value stream can consist of a single series of processes or multiple series of processes.

For example, a company that has a single sequence of macro processes in its value stream would be a commodity producer such as a coal mine. Core business processes can be represented by a single chain as shown in the figure below, thus it would have one value stream.

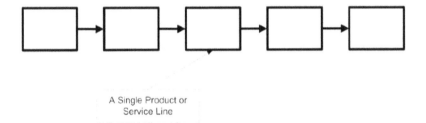

A Single Product or
Service Line

Value Stream for Single Product or Service

A company that has numerous value streams for delivering goods and services would be a telecommunications company such as Telstra, which provides a range of products and services. Core or primary business processes can be represented by a number of product or service streams that transgress across the individual functions of the business as shown in the figure on the next page.

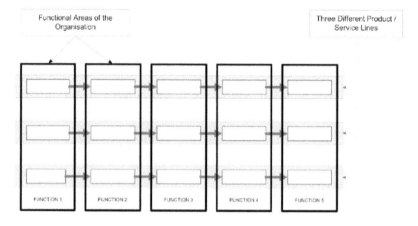

Value Streams for Multiple Products or Services

Value Stream Analysis

'The value chain focused organisation is one that focuses on multiple processes from an end-to-end perspective. An organisation with this approach moves away from the traditional hierarchical structure to a structure based on a horizontal process flow. Primary relationships are customer - supplier based, and the style of leadership shifts from authoritarian to participative. Business leaders and managers aim to establish a seamless link between processes through optimising exchanges and interfaces. The interface between processes and customers will be the driving force for decision-making and behaviour.'

George Lee Sye (From Process Alchemy 2nd Edition)

Value Stream Analysis

Value Stream Analysis (VSA) is a process for:

1. Documenting the flow of information, materials and activities through each of the product or service value streams used by a company to generate profits; and

2. Analysing the actual performance of that process with respect to the needs of the customer and the business as well as other efficiency metrics.

It can most effectively be used following the development of a SIPOC.

Why would we do VSA?

The desired outcome is to distinguish value adding from non-value adding activities and to understand the existence of waste as a product goes through a process.

It differs from typical process mapping used in traditional Six Sigma in a number of ways.

1. A value stream map usually represents a process at a much higher level than a process map or flowchart. It usually covers the process from receiving raw materials through to delivery of finished products.

2. It displays a broader range of information by representing a combination of information, material and production flow as units pass through the process.

3. A value stream map helps to make waste in a process more obvious.

The Value Stream Map

VSA involves the use of simple graphics and icons that are assembled in such a way that the 'value stream' for a particular product or service can be understood.

This assembly of icons is referred to as a 'value stream map' as shown in the following example.

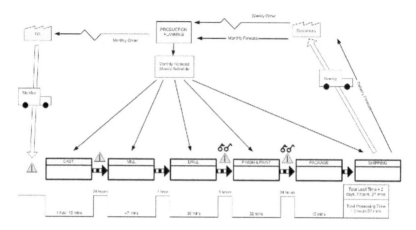

Value Stream Map Example

You will notice in this particular example, boxes represent the process and the sequence from 'casting' to 'shipping' is laid out at a macro level.

The flow of information is indicated in various ways, and a series of measurements are captured at the lower part of the map.

Value Stream Map Icons

To understand a value stream map, you must first understand the standard icons and notations used in the map. The following diagram depicts some of the most commonly used icons.

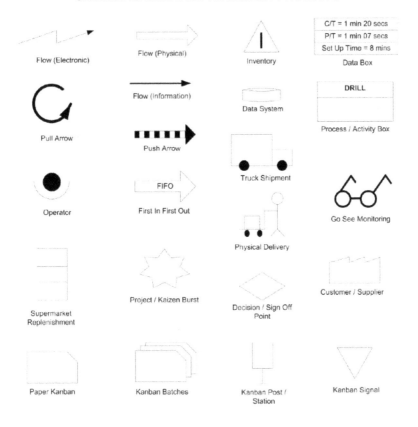

VSM Icons / Notations

Dimensions Of Value Stream Measurement

There are three principal dimensions for measuring the performance of value streams:

1. Horizontally through the value stream as customer needs are interpreted

2. Vertically down into the value stream as the business needs are interpreted

3. In the space between process steps where the factory of waste conceals itself

1. Horizontally Through the Value Stream

This dimension relates to how effective one is in meeting the needs of the customer. The measure has application across the business as a whole and for each of the functional areas within the business who all have internal customers. Effectiveness measures can also be linked to the requirements that suppliers must meet in order for you to meet your customer's requirements.

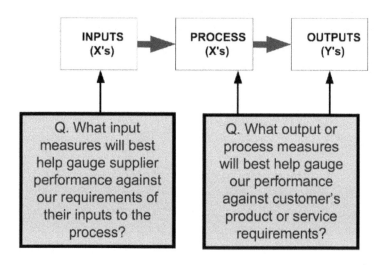

Questions to Identify Effectiveness Measures

KEY HORIZONTAL METRICS

As you will find, a number of metrics from the Six Sigma toolkit are designed to help you understand and identify major effectiveness issues.

These include:

Cycle Time: The time that passes between the start and completion of a process or process step (eg: leave processing, Software Loading etc).

Yield: A measure for determining process performance based on the proportion of units that are defect free.

Final Yield: A measure for determining the proportion of units produced that are defect free at the end of the process.

Rolled Throughput Yield: A measure for determining the performance of the process as a whole, taking into consideration yield at each step along the way.

Process Sigma Quality Level: A measure for determining the performance of a process based on the number of Defects Per Million Opportunities (DPMO) produced and how this number relates to variation.

2. Vertically Down into the Value Stream

This relates to how efficient one is in the use of resources, linked to the needs of the business. Efficiency measures mostly focus on use of time, money and physical resources.

KEY VERTICAL METRICS

These include:

Cost Per Unit: The actual cost of producing one unit of a product. Units can be defined by weight (e.g. one tonne of product) or any other product relevant metric.

Units Per Hour Worked: This metric takes into consideration total hours worked by employees and units produced per worked hour (whereas units per hour or cycle time to produce one unit do not).

Productivity Measures: In economics, productivity refers to actual output from production processes per unit of input. For example, labor productivity may be typically measured as a ratio of units (the output) per labor-hour (the input).

A vitally important point to remember – 'In the absence of effectiveness measures (customer focused), efficiency measures will drive a silo mentality and ultimately result in lost efficiency across the company'.

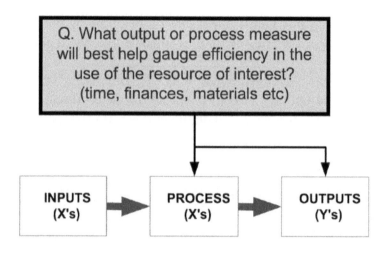

Questions to Identify Efficiency Measures

3. In the Process Where the Hidden Factory of Waste Exists

As you will find, a number of metrics from the Lean toolkit are perfectly designed to help you identify major efficiency issues, predominantly those associated with speed and flow. These are often missed by standard productivity measures mentioned previously.

KEY EFFICIENCY METRICS

These include:

Processing Time: The time taken to complete one cycle of a designated activity or operation in a work process.

Process Cycle Efficiency: PCE is a measure of overall process health and is calculated as a percentage by dividing value added time by total lead time (refer to Little's Law). A PCE of 25 percent is considered to be world class, although it will vary according to different applications.

Little's Law: Sometimes referred to as the 'law of velocity', Little's Law is the equation used to calculate total lead time. It simply involves dividing total work in progress by the average completion rate. Reducing total lead time involves increasing capacity or average completion rate, or reducing work in progress.

VA/NVA Ratio: This is a ratio that is calculated by comparing the amount of value added (VA) time to non value added (NVA) time in a work process.

Set Up Time: Time taken to actually set up for production of a particular unit. This becomes particularly relevant when changing dies in a production line that produces multiple types of products.

Inventory Turns: The number of times inventory is consumed in a specific period of time.

Inventory: A measurement of parts, products or material that sit for a period of time in a production line, store or stockpile. Inventory includes raw materials, work in progress as well as finished or final products.

Queueing Time: The length of time a unit waits in line before work commences on it. Also referred to as wait time.

Using V.S.A. In Project Identification

A process owner can create a framework for selecting excellent projects using Value Stream Analysis in this way:

1. Develop the Value Stream Map

2. Identify key value stream performance measures - you may find that a SIPOC of the process helps you understand the requirements placed on the process by the customer and the business as well as the requirements placed on suppliers by the process itself – these provide

clues as to some of the key measures to include in your Value Stream Map

3. Obtain performance data for key measures

4. Select and prioritise projects based on the greatest opportunities for value growth according to how well the process is performing against these measures

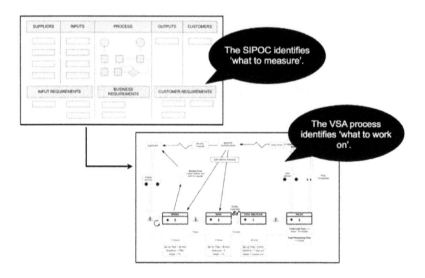

Project Selection with VSA

Chapter 4 - Business Driver Analysis

Business Drivers

This approach to identifying margin improving opportunities is based on understanding the relationship between business drivers, processes and organisational value.

The higher level business goals or objectives of an organisation will determine what the key drivers of the business are.

These key drivers will determine your core business processes – those that actually create value that is linked to high level business goals, and those that enable (or support) the creation of value. Within each of these processes, there will be elements that drive operating cost, capital expenditure, working capital, revenue and risk exposure.

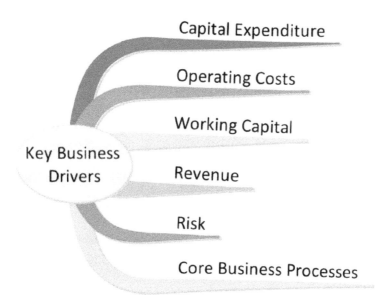

Understanding Key Business Drivers

Operating cost, capital expenditure, working capital, revenue and risk exposure are consequences or benefits (depending upon which way you look at it) of which the business itself is a customer. At the macro level, these will drive the commercial value of your business.

I know you're wondering how does knowing this fit in with our discussion around identifying opportunities for profit expansion? Hang in there, that will become clearer as you read more.

Continual Improvement Is The Key To Success

While 'defect reduction' has traditionally been the primary focal point of 'continual improvement' or 'business improvement' in large corporations, *not* all profit improving opportunities have to be focused on reducing cost or defects.

While product quality improvement can impact both revenue and costs, we can and should have a much broader focus.

All of your work to improve your business should be aligned to the higher level objectives of your business. Without doubt, the most critical of these will be financial. So if you're able to target those things that drive the financials of your business, then you'll be in a good position to make an even more valuable contribution to your business as well as all of its stakeholders.

There are principally only five areas of focus for your improvement efforts:

1. Reducing your PER UNIT COST OF PRODUCTION;

2. Reducing the level of WORKING CAPITAL tied up in the business;

3. Reducing CAPITAL EXPENDITURE;

4. Reducing RISK EXPOSURE; and

5. Increasing REVENUE by increasing throughput or sales volume.

These focal points can be *problem* driven (waste, re-works, bad debts, increasing cost of capital, short equipment life cycles, exposure to hazards, bottlenecks etc), or a *proactive* approach targeting the biggest drivers of cost, working capital, capital expenditure or revenue (such as cycle time, inventories, plant life cycles, throughput, sales volume, lead generation etc).

The most effective work I have observed in this area for medium to larger organisation has begun with analysis of specific areas or functions within the business. For example plant maintenance or logistics can undertake the approach shown next within their own area, while production does something similar in their area.

For smaller businesses this may or may not be relevant. It might just make sense to focus on the business as a single function.

The Most Common Drivers

The following table presents some examples of common types of drivers to consider when thinking about where to focus your improvement efforts.

BUSINESS COMPONENT	DRIVERS
Capital Expenditure	Equipment and Plant Life Cycles (computers, office machines, vehicles etc), Technology Ownership and Access Policies
Working Capital	Trade Debtors / Stock Inventory / Parts Inventory / Work in Progress or WIP
Operating Costs	Power / Labour / Equipment Hire / Fuel / Consumables / Phone Expenses / Rent / Subscriptions / Maintenance / Consultants / Venue Hire / Travel and Accommodation
Revenue	Production Volumes / Production Cycle Time / Delivery Cycle Time / Lead Generation / Sales Volume / Sale Conversation Rates
Risk	Exposure to Hazards / Strategic or Business Risks / Missing Business Opportunities

Let me ask you this. If you were able to affect these drivers in some positive way, how would that impact your business?

I'll make an educated guess and say the impact would be seen in financial results. For example if you were able to reduce the cycle time to receive payment from your customers (accounts receivable), that would increase your cash reserves. If you were able to reduce your internet and phone costs, that would increase your profitability. If you could reduce the level of inventory you held and still meet the demand of your customers, that would reduce how much money you had sitting there doing nothing in the store, does that make sense?

Every single driver can be positively impacted! Either through applying some improvement methodology like Lean Thinking, or through implementing some appropriate operating strategy such as Joint Venture development or Internet Marketing. You just need to:

a. Know where to focus for the greatest impact; and

b. Become *way more* innovative and curious about what is out there that you don't know yet.

Let's talk about how we might be more scientific in how we go about choosing our focal points for improvement. The approach discussed over following pages is *one* of the methods we use in our work with clients who are intent on implementing a business improvement initiative such as Lean Six Sigma.

Identifying The Right Focal Points

This process for identifying potential areas of improvement for your business is quite simple. All you have to do is ...

FOCUS on a functional area of your business (if it makes sense to focus on production, sales, accounting and admin, supply etc); and

Ask the RIGHT QUESTIONS (of the right people, important if you have employees).

The right type of question will focus discussion and generate relevant ideas. People already know the answers, all you have to do is extract them.

Let me offer you some suggestions as to the types of questions you might ask.

Asking The Right Questions

Let's assume we've chosen a single business component as our focal point (i.e. capital expenditure, working capital, operating cost, revenue or risk).

The first question to ask is designed to identify the drivers for this component.

Q. What drives [insert a business component - e.g. working capital] within the functional area we're focused on?

You could also generalise with your business, rather than limit it to a functional area and simply ask ... 'What drives [e.g. working capital] in our business?

You simply brainstorm the *logical* answers. Let's look at an example. For 'working capital' we might get answers like:

- Trade debtors

- Stock inventory

- Parts inventory

- Work in progress

Each of these drive working capital in the business in some way.

FINANCIAL ITEM	DRIVERS
WORKING CAPITAL	Trade Debtors / Stock Inventory / Parts Inventory / Work in Progress
Primary Driver:	
Contributing Variables:	

We then choose the driver we believe to have the biggest impact by asking:

Q. Which of these drivers has the biggest impact on [insert the business component - e.g. working capital in this case]?

Continuing the example, for a business that requires machinery and vehicles to function we might find that:

'Parts Inventory' is the biggest driver of 'Working Capital'

Our assumption is that a *decrease in parts inventory* will help *reduce the level of working capital* tied up in the business.

FINANCIAL ITEM	DRIVERS
WORKING CAPITAL	Trade Debtors / Stock Inventory / Parts Inventory / Work in Progress
Primary Driver:	Parts Inventory
Contributing Variables:	

There will be occasions when this particular question is better answered when we understand the values for each of the drivers identified in the previous question. That means a bit of data collection might be necessary.

Let's dig down a bit deeper into the 'cause and effect' relationship by looking at next level variables. We simply ask a question like:

Q. What *variables* have the greatest impact on [insert the variable - e.g. parts inventory]?

In the case we might get answers like:

- Time to receive parts

- Average unit cost

- Inventory accuracy level

All we are doing is breaking down to lower level variables that contribute to our business drivers. The process is basically a way of understanding *cause and effect* relationships.

In this case, our logic is that movements in time to receive inventory, average cost per unit and accuracy levels all have an impact on working capital that's tied up in parts inventory. All we need to do is work out which of these variables to focus our energies on in the first instance.

FINANCIAL ITEM	DRIVERS
WORKING CAPITAL	Trade Debtors / Stock Inventory / Parts Inventory / Work in Progress
Primary Driver:	Parts Inventory
Contributing Variables:	Time to receive parts / Average unit cost / Inventory accuracy level

By the way, this question can be asked multiple times to help drill down even lower, although that's not always necessary.

Continuing with the example, when you've chosen your most important variables, you then ask the next question.

Q. What improvement focus now makes sense?

In your answer, use a phrase that includes a verb such as reduce, minimise or increase etc. In our example, we might come up with answers like:

- *Reduce* lead times for parts supply

- *Reduce* average cost per unit

- *Increase* inventory accuracy

Our logic is that a reduction or increase, depending on the variable, will have a positive impact on

Q. What improvement level would be a *reasonable* target?

Specific goals can be defined at this time. Where there is insufficient information to define straight away, these can be defined later.

In our example, we might come up with answers like:

- *Reduce* lead times for parts supply by *10 percent*

- *Reduce* average cost per unit by *2 percent*

- *Increase* inventory accuracy from *80 percent to 90 percent*

Now it's simply a matter of understanding the financial impact (on working capital) that would occur if we were to make these levels of improvement. It's this impact on the key element you originally started with that helps you decide where to put your energies.

Ask yourself ...

Q. If that level of improvement was achieved, what value would that add to business?

Because you are trying to impact a financial item such as working capital or revenue, the impact is estimated in financial terms. If *risk* happened to be your focus, then you'd simply use whatever metric you determine risk by.

In our example, we might come up with answers like:

1. *Reduce* lead times for parts supply by *25 percent*

- Business Value: We could reduce stock levels by approximately 20 percent which would equate to $xxxx less working capital

2. *Reduce* average cost per unit by *2 percent* -

- Business Value: If there achieved, it would translate into $xxxx less working capital

3. *Increase* inventory accuracy from *80 percent to 90 percent*

- Business Value: We could reduce stock levels by approximately 10 percent which would equate to $xxx, plus reduce air freight expenses by $xxx

This understanding of financial impact ultimately helps you prioritise all of the opportunities in front of you.

The outcomes of this discussion might look something like this.

FINANCIAL ITEM	DRIVERS		
WORKING CAPITAL	Trade Debtors / Stock Inventory / Parts Inventory / Work in Progress		
Primary Driver:	Parts Inventory		
Contributing Variables:	Time to receive parts / Average unit cost / Inventory accuracy level		
3 Potential Projects:	Reduce Lead Times	Reduce Avg. Unit Purchase Costs	Increase Inventory Accuracy
Reasonable Improvement Level	25% reduction on average	2% reduction on average	Increased from 80% to 90%
Value to the Business	Reduce stock levels by approx. 20 percent equating to $xxxx less working capital	If there achieved, it would translate into $xxxx less working capital	Reduced airfreight costs of $xxx pa Reduce stock levels by approx. 10 percent equating to $xxx less working capital
Process Owner	Michelle Stevens (Supply Supervisor)	Steve Jacobs (Purchasing Supervisor)	Fred Dutton (Store Supervisor)

At the end of this questioning process it's possible to create a list of potential improvement projects that are all linked to the higher level objectives of your business.

A Revenue Generating Example

The outcome of a revenue focused process might look something like this.

FINANCIAL ITEM	DRIVERS		
REVENUE	Production Volume / Sales Volume / Gross Margin / US exchange rates		
Primary Driver:	Sales volume		
Contributing Variables:	Internet sales / Promotion conversion rates /		
3 Potential Projects:	Increase internet based sales volume	Increase promotion event conversion rates	
Reasonable Improvement Level	10% increase over avg. monthly in 2010	Increase from 22% to 25%	
Value to the Business	Increased annual revenue by $192k	Increased annual revenue by $350k	
Process Owner	Jeffrey Roth (Marketing Manager)	Stephanie Jones (Event Management)	

Business Driver Trees

The cause & effect relationship between revenue, working capital, cost and their drivers can be explored much deeper with the development of 'Driver Trees'.

A driver tree, as used by many of the larger organisations, is simply a 'tree diagram'. It is one of the seven management and planning tools described by Japanese contributor to quality concepts, Shigeru Mizuno.

For more information about driver trees, you should download and ready my eBook titled *Creating Wealth In Business* - http://www.georgeleesye.com/books

At the time of writing this book, *Creating Wealth In Business* was the 3rd most downloaded Business and Economics book on iTunes.

Chapter 5 - Analysing for Constraints

Of Course It's Constrained

Where the primary value chain has at least one of the processes in the sequence operating at one hundred percent of its capacity, it's constrained. It *cannot* produce more without significant change.

What's more, the other processes within the sequence are obviously not operating at their designed capacity, and are therefore under utilised.

Let's look at a simplistic example.

The diagram below shows a primary value chain consisting of five processes in a sequence. Each process has been measured for current (actual) throughput in units. This figure has been converted into a percentage of the designed maximum throughput (capacity) of the process.

The measurement used is not important as the analysis is based on percentages.

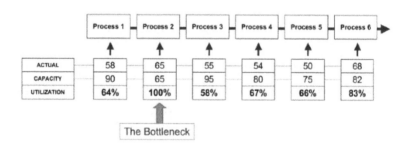

Process Bottlenecks

From the figures shown, we can see that process two is operating at one hundred percent of its designed capacity, hence it is the constraint (or bottleneck) to any increased throughput. Unless its capacity is increased, the throughput of the system *cannot* be increased.

To Improve Or To Replace

I want to share a story with you as told to me by a good friend during a Lean Six Sigma seminar I facilitated in South Africa.

Some years ago, a US based technology company found that an automatic soldering machine used in the process of manufacturing components for computers was operating with a defect rate of about 40 percent. The 60 percent *non*-defect rate was sufficient to ensure that supply met customer demands.

The attitude of the company was that the cost of defective components wasted was negligible so no action was taken to correct or reduce the level of waste. However, over a relatively short period of time demand for components outgrew capacity, so the bottleneck in the system, the soldering machine, needed to be addressed.

A case was put forward and the company purchased a larger capacity soldering machine. The older machine was subsequently sold to a Japanese technology company. The new machine had a much higher capacity so supply once again exceeded demand.

As we all know, the growth in technology use and application has continued to grow exponentially. It wasn't long before the company's ability to supply components could no longer meet demand, and a study showed that the larger capacity machine produced ... surprise surprise ... a similar defect rate to the machine it replaced. The bottleneck had been removed, however, the defect rate of about 40 percent had not been changed.

It was only a matter of time before demand caught up to the non-defect capacity of the machine. So now a case could be put forward to buy a larger or a second soldering machine. However the company decided to investigate what had happened to the first machine that they had sold and shipped overseas to Japan.

What they found was that the soldering process had been improved in the machine to the point where it produced defects measured in the parts per billion. The Japanese company had virtually eliminated defects from the process. The machine still processed the same number of units, however the non-defect capacity was increased some 40 percent.

Hmmm, interesting.

To Invest Capital Or Not To Invest Capital

Another story worth sharing is that of a large open cut mine in the Asia Pacific area.

The mining division had a daily target to move 240,000 tonnes of material. With a waste (dirt not containing ore) to ore strip ratio of about 1:1, this equated to some 120,000 tonnes of ore containing material each day.

The fleet of 28 haul trucks were averaging about 7,800 tonnes per day each, which equated to about 218,000 tonnes per day of actual material moved. The target was not being achieved. The obvious solution was to buy an additional three haul trucks which mathematically showed that the target could be exceeded.

I am not sure if you know what a haul truck is, but I can tell you they cost a lot of money to buy and are quite expensive to run and maintain. In this scenario, a credible case to expend capital and purchase three trucks was submitted *and* approved.

Fortunately, a new mining manager took over production during that period. His experience in the industry served to help him recognise that something wasn't right in the mine pit. He analysed what was happening and found that approximately 30 percent of the time the trucks were in the pit, they spent in queues at either shovels or at the crushers where material was prepared for further processing.

His solution – take five trucks *out* of the system and change the fleet management system. The action resulted in a better work rate for the remaining trucks and the target of 240,000 tonnes per day was *easily* exceeded. In addition, the capital expenditure was not made, and the cost of running these five trucks was saved.

Caterpillar Haul Truck

The reason why I tell these stories is because of the lessons we can learn from them.

Firstly, when addressing a bottleneck or constraint, a company has a number of choices it can make to treat it.

1. As a CAPITAL PROJECT – build or buy larger capacity; or

2. As an IMPROVEMENT PROJECT – increase non-defective capacity through studying and treating the critical input and process variables that impact defect and throughput rates.

When deciding which path to take, it makes sense to involve a cross section of personnel from both engineering and the business improvement team. Both paths should be considered.

Not all bottlenecks require capital expenditure. The capacity of a process *can* be increased if waste is reduced or eliminated.

On the other hand, not all bottlenecks can be eliminated through process improvement. For example, if you want to pump fuel faster from a tank, you might need to buy a new pump and larger hose.

Chapter 6 - Analysing Customer Related Performance

The Process Sigma Quality Scale

If someone said to you that 99 percent of their products were defect free, what would you think? Sounds good doesn't it? What about 99.9 percent quality, now that's fantastic. What would be the effect of 99.9 percent quality on our lives?

Consider the following examples of what 99.9 percent looks like:

- 291 pacemaker operations in the United States will be performed incorrectly this year

- 1 new born baby would be given to the wrong parents every day in Australia

- 4.9 million articles would be mishandled each year by Australia Post

- 133,335 documents will be misplaced by the Australian Taxation Office each year

- 58,500 credit cards will fail to work when paying for goods

- Webster's dictionary will have 315 misspellings in it

- More than 4,000 parts will fail on every Boeing 747 aircraft

Would 99.9 percent be 'good enough' for you if you experienced an error in the scenarios above? More importantly, would 99 percent, or even 99.9 percent, be good enough for your customers in respect of your products or services?

When we hear that a product is a 'Six Sigma' product then we know that its quality is excellent, and the probability that it has a defect is extremely low. The table below demonstrates this by showing a comparison between 90 percent quality, 99 percent quality and 'Six Sigma' quality.

Item Measured	90% Quality	99% Quality	Six Sigma Quality
Downtime for an item of heavy machinery in a 30 day month	72.0 hours	7.2 hours	0.14688 minutes
Defectives vehicles per 100,000 vehicles sold	10,000	1,000	< 1
Received parts not matching orders per 250,000 orders	25,000	2,500	< 1
Period of unsafe drinking water each day	2.4 hours	14.4 minutes	0.004896 minutes
Period without electricity each week	16.8 hours	1.68 hours	0.034272 minutes

Quality Percentage Examples

There are many industries where a Six Sigma result would not be good enough – pharmaceutical, aviation, space aeronautics, medical and the like. Much higher results (measured in the parts per billion) must be sustained where the consequences of a defect are unacceptable.

One of the unique features of Six Sigma is its quality measurement scale. The designers of the scale recognised the resistance that is normally experienced in western culture when there is talk of zero defects. Tell your staff that you want zero defects and you are likely to get comments like – 'It can't be done' or in Australia, 'You've got to be joking mate'. The Six Sigma quality measurement scale acknowledges this likely resistance and helps to overcome it in three ways:

1. It provides the foundation for setting and achieving improvement milestones, and helps create a culture of continual improvement;

2. It measures performance against customers' requirements; and

3. It provides a basis for consistent performance comparison.

The Sigma quality level, or process sigma, is calculated on the basis of Defects Per Million Opportunities (DPMO). When we talk about opportunities, we are referring to opportunities for a defect per unit produced.

You will notice on the measurement scale, that as you achieve a higher Sigma Quality level, DPMO (Defects Per Million Opportunities) are reduced exponentially. You may also notice that process yield (proportion of units defect free) improvements get smaller.

Sigma Quality Level	Process Yield (%)	Defects Per Million Opportunities
6	99.99966	3.4
5	99.977	233
4	99.38	6,210
3	93.32	66,807
2	69.15	308,537
1	30.85	690,000

Process Sigma Quality Levels

At the 'Six Sigma' quality level, a process (in the short term) would only produce 3.4 defects per million opportunities (see the notation below) , which equates to a process yield of 99.99966 percent.

Prior to starting a 'Six Sigma' quality initiative, many of an organisation's processes will operate at a quality level of between one and three sigma. It is often quite startling for process owners to find out their process produces no less than 66,000 defects for every million opportunities. Whilst this level of performance may have served them well to this point in time, there are organisations out there working hard at reducing their level of defects.

> **Statistics Notation:** *The area beyond plus and minus six sigma under a normal curve equates to 2 parts-per-billion. Six Sigma assumes that over the long term a process will shift and drift by as much as 1.5 sigma. You will find that 3.4 ppm equates to the area beyond plus and minus 4.5 sigma and this value is used to discuss short term snapshots of process performance.*

The sigma quality scale provides a useful approach to evaluating process performance against customer requirements. This is the only method for calculating your sigma quality level (commonly referred to as Process Sigma) when you have more than one critical-to-quality characteristic against which you wish to measure performance, as other methods based on distributions of data can only accommodate the analysis of a single product or service characteristic.

Some of the reasons why it may be value adding to calculate process sigma are:

- It forces the discussion around what a defect is in the eyes of a customer.

- To establish a baseline performance against which future performance can be compared.

Process Sigma Terms

To calculate the sigma quality level of your process, you first need to familiarise yourself with the following terms:

A Unit

This is the thing or item produced or processed, or the service provided (for example – trucks repaired, online web sites, orders from customers, flight seat booked etc).

A Defect

This is any critical-to-quality (CTQ) characteristic that does not meet customers' requirements. The key word here is critical to quality in the eyes of the customer. When defects are defined they must be mutually exclusive so that we do not get duplication when counting defects.

Defects are those events that if they occur, would probably cause the customer to consider the product or service to be defective. Defects can be specified in respect of a product (for example - torn upholstery, outside the specified width, web site not available etc), or in respect of a process (for example - time to deliver longer than specified time, repair time exceeding 24 hours, order details taken incorrectly the first time, incorrect ticket destination etc).

A Defect Opportunity

This is any opportunity for a unit to not meet the CTQ requirements of the customer.

This answers the question – 'How many opportunities would there be for a customer to be dissatisfied with our product or service, and therefore consider it to be defective? It is essentially the number of defects that can appear *for each unit* produced. It *is not* the number of opportunities that exists *in a process* to create a defect!

DPMO

Defects per million opportunities [for a defect to occur].

The Calculation

You start the process of identifying your sigma quality level by using a simple equation to calculate DPMO (defects per million opportunities).

Once you have made the calculation (DPMO), you then convert the result to a 'Short Term Sigma' value using the conversion chart shown on the following pages. Equations are shown in the tabled example presented next.

Some keys points to remember:

The number of defect opportunities must stay constant before and after improvement if the comparison of results is to be useful – remember that any convention, even if flawed, can be useful if used consistently

Where many defects might be listed, these may be categorised into one major defect heading (i.e. for a motor vehicle manufacturer, CTQ defects associated with the engine, gear box and differential could be categorised under the main heading of 'Drive Train Failure')

Approximating Process Sigma

The worksheet shown on the following page is useful for approximating Process Sigma for any process. As you are making your calculation on the basis of a sample of units, then you are only approximating the sigma quality level of the entire population of units. The larger the sample size, the more likely it is you will be close to the true sigma quality level. The example shows the calculation for both DPMO and Process Yield, however as both generate the same Process Sigma result I have focused these notes on DPMO.

Using the Worksheet

To approximate the Process Sigma of a process, simply follow the prompts shown in the left hand column. The example shows the Process Sigma calculation for the 'coffee making' process of a small café.

SELECTING GREAT IMPROVEMENT PROJECTS

Step 1. Specify the process being analysed.	Coffee Making
Step 2. Define what a UNIT is.	A cup of coffee
Step 3. Make a list of the DEFECTS that could occur in a unit as determined by the expectations of the CUSTOMER, Q. What would constitute a DEFECT in that unit?	A defect occurs when: (a) Product delivered does not match order (b) Dirty cup (c) Liquid content is not within 5mm of the top of the cup (d) Time between order and delivery is longer than 2 minutes
Step 4. Calculate the defect opportunities per unit (**O**) by adding the total number of defects identified in step 3.	Every time a customer buys a cup of coffee, any one of the 4 listed defects can occur. **O** = 4
Step 5. Count the number of units (**N**) analysed.	N = 340
Step 6. From the units in step 5, determine the total number of defects (**D**) of the type described in step 3 that were observed.	**D** = 27
Step 7a. Calculate DPMO using the equation: $1,000,000 \times \dfrac{D}{N \times O}$ Where : D = Number of defects N = Number of units counted O = Number of opportunities per unit OR	$1,000,000 \times \dfrac{27}{340 \times 4}$ = 19,853
Step 7b. Calculate Process Yield using the equation: $(1 - \dfrac{D}{N \times O}) \times 100$ Where : D = Number of defects N = Number of units counted O = Number of opportunities per unit	$(1 - \dfrac{27}{340 \times 4}) \times 100$ = 98%
Step 8. Convert DPMO or Process Yield to a Short Term Process Sigma using the conversation table.	Short term Sigma Quality Level = 3.5

8 Step Process Sigma Quality Calculation

The table for converting 'DPMO' or 'Process Yield' into a Process Sigma value is shown on the following pages.

Process Sigma Conversation Table

To convert DPMO or Process Yield into a Short Term Process Sigma value, simply locate the relevant DPMO or Yield value and identify the corresponding Process Sigma Quality value.

DPMO	Yield	Process Sigma (ST)
3.4	99.99966%	6
5	99.9995%	5.9
8	99.9992%	5.8
10	99.9990%	5.7
20	99.9980%	5.6
30	99.9970%	5.5
40	99.9960%	5.4
70	99.9930%	5.3
100	99.9900%	5.2
150	99.9850%	5.1
230	99.9770%	5
330	99.9670%	4.9
480	99.9520%	4.8
680	99.9320%	4.7
960	99.9040%	4.6
1,350	99.8650%	4.5
1,860	99.8140%	4.4
2,550	99.7450%	4.3
3,460	99.6540%	4.2
4,660	99.5340%	4.1
6,210	99.3790%	4
8,190	99.1810%	3.9
10,700	98.9300%	3.8
13,900	98.6100%	3.7
17,800	98.2200%	3.6
22,700	97.7300%	3.5
28,700	97.1300%	3.4
35,900	96.4100%	3.3
44,600	95.5400%	3.2
54,800	94.5200%	3.1
66,800	93.3200%	3
80,800	91.9200%	2.9
96,800	90.3200%	2.8

Short Term Process Sigma Quality Level Conversion Table

(Continued on next page)

DPMO	Yield	Process Sigma (ST)
115,000	88.5000%	2.7
135,000	86.5000%	2.6
158,000	84.2000%	2.5
184,000	81.6000%	2.4
212,000	78.8000%	2.3
242,000	75.8000%	2.2
274,000	72.6000%	2.1
308,000	69.2000%	2
344,000	65.6000%	1.9
382,000	61.8000%	1.8
420,000	58.0000%	1.7
460,000	54.0000%	1.6
500,000	50.0000%	1.5
540,000	46.0000%	1.4
570,000	43.0000%	1.3
610,000	39.0000%	1.2
650,000	35.0000%	1.1
690,000	31.0000%	1
720,000	28.0000%	0.9
750,000	25.0000%	0.8
780,000	22.0000%	0.7
810,000	19.0000%	0.6
840,000	16.0000%	0.5
860,000	14.0000%	0.4
880,000	12.0000%	0.3
900,000	10.0000%	0.2
920,000	8.0000%	0.1

Short Term Process Sigma Quality Level Conversion Table

(Continued from previous page)

Chapter 7 - A Question You Have To Ask

Who generates improvement ideas?

Well ... who does?

Let's see if we can answer that question like this.

Top Down, Bottom Up

There are two ways to approach the generation of ideas. One way is to open up the pipeline to every person in the organisation. Let's refer to this as 'bottom up' idea generation.

Another way to approach idea generation is to have business leaders / managers generate ideas for improving the business. Let's refer to this as 'top down' idea generation.

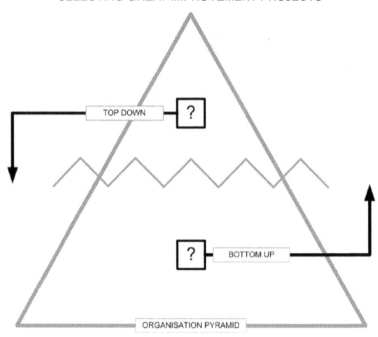

Bottom Up and Top Down Idea Generation

We all know that ... so what? Okay, let's explore this a bit more.

Bottom Up Idea Generation

In this approach *any* employee submits ideas for improving the business. Many of the companies we work with have an online system that supports the process associated with submitting and tracking ideas.

So why would a company undertake this approach? There are a number of benefits in taking this approach including these.

1. Employees are *actively involved* in the business improvement initiative; they feel a part of it as opposed to it being something that belongs to business leaders.

2. Employees have the opportunity to make change where it impacts them *personally*; this can lead to them developing a positive association with the business improvement initiative.

3. There is a greater probability of building a 'continual improvement culture' when *all employees are involved* in a process that consistently causes *them* to ask questions such as 'How can I do this better?' or 'How can this be improved?'

While there are benefits, there is also a downside if this is your *only* approach.

1. Ideas will mostly be driven by that which causes *problems or pain* for the employee. This is only one half of the equation as ideas should also be generated in areas where there are no problems, only opportunities to proactively go to the next level of performance.

2. Ideas will be actual *solutions* to the problem in most cases. We all have a natural tendency to jump straight to a solution, and a key principle behind successful process improvement methodologies is that solutions are generated after proper analysis. Having said that, it does not mean that their solution is not the right one as many low hanging fruit have been captured by businesses using this approach.

3. Ideas are not usually generated in conjunction with business planning and achievement of the *company's* strategic objectives.

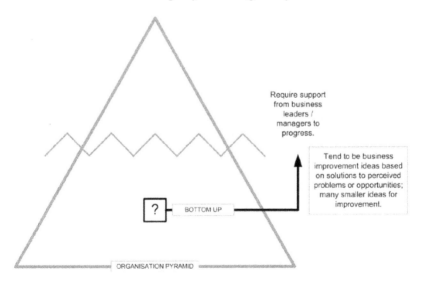

Bottom Up Idea Generation

If you do take on this method of idea generation, let me offer you some tips.

1. When an employee generates an idea, they must have feedback. A behaviour that will absolutely kill this approach is to have ideas generated and they just disappear into the void, never to be seen or heard of again.

2. Be aware that you can easily create what I would call a 'digital stockpile'. That is a list of ideas that you cannot deal with due to capacity constraints. The process for dealing with ideas must be well thought out and 'lean' in that ideas can move through in a reasonable time frame.

Top Down Idea Generation

In this approach, business leaders and managers generate ideas for improving the business.

Regardless of the method used, ideas *should* be more strategic and have a greater impact on the business plan. Companies that do this well take a very systematic approach to scheduling and facilitating idea generation and selection.

The benefits of this approach include these:

1. Projects usually have a much stronger *connection to the business plan* and result in greater progress towards achieving business goals.

2. The involvement of leaders and managers in choosing projects is more likely to result in *them taking an active role* in project progress.

3. The projects are more likely to be based on gap creation or gap identification. The involvement of employees in developing solutions for closing these gaps result in *more obvious collaboration* between

leaders and employees, and empowerment of those who work with the process.

The downside for you if this is your *only* approach to idea generation include:

1. All ideas come from the leaders with *little involvement of employees*. Employees could perceive that the initiative is not theirs but one that belongs to someone else. The involvement of employees in selecting and implementing solutions is an essential component in addressing this risk.

2. Many of the *nagging issues for employees* may never be addressed. The opportunity to build positive associations with business improvement may well be missed.

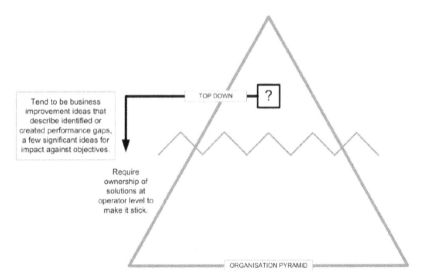

Top Down Idea Generation

Who To Allocate Projects To

Each of the different approaches produce different types of improvement ideas. The improvement ideas generated by leadership team members *should* be more strategic, often more complex in nature, and in the majority of cases do not indicate how the improvement will be made (the solution) but rather what the desired improvement is (to reduce, to improve, to increase etc).

For these reasons, it will usually be more appropriate to allocate these projects to a highly trained business improvement practitioner such as a Lean Six Sigma Green Belt or Black belt. The work could involve more complex analysis and the use of advanced tools, as well as the facilitation of a cross-functional project team.

On the other hand, ideas generated by employees in general will tend to lend themselves to more common tools and skills. Solutions can be implemented using regular 'project management' techniques.

Where solutions are not known, basic tools and skills of process improvement and problem solving may suffice. For these reasons, projects may well be allocated to a project manager, or a facilitator with basic business improvement training, or even returned to the originator to lead the work.

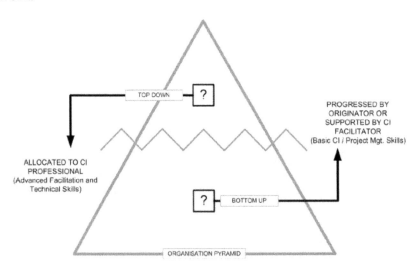

Project Allocation

Some Closing Thoughts

I have facilitated idea generation sessions on many occasions where the people involved were a combination of (a) leadership team members, and (b) supervisory and operational staff.

When these two groupings work independently of each other, I almost always see two radically different lists of ideas; some very strategically focused, others focused on solving problems.

For this reason you must think carefully about *who* is going to be involved in the process of idea generation and make sure it fits your overall business improvement strategy and targeted outcomes.

Okay, that's enough about identification of improvement opportunities, let's talk about the selection of projects.

Chapter 8 - Choosing Wisely

The selection of improvement projects using some sound scientific methodology is *critical* to the success of business improvement as a business strategy, *and* in ensuring improvement practitioners (Black Belts and Green Belts) are able to learn and continually reinforce the skills of Lean and Six Sigma through successful project execution.

The framework provided for choosing projects in this book is established on the basis of three simple selection principles:

- Firstly projects being undertaken must contribute to the needs of the business.

- Secondly projects formally undertaken using a specific methodology [such as Lean and Six Sigma] *must* meet criteria associated with the needs of that methodology.

- And thirdly, those that are undertaken should be prioritised in order of the potential value they might bring to the business.

These principles are aligned with the need to only undertake projects that impact positively on business objectives, and provide the foundation for development of business improvement professionals within your business such as Lean Six Sigma Black Belts and Green Belts.

Screening Questions For All Opportunities

All improvement projects undertaken must add *value* to the business in some way. This is one of the most important factors behind the success of *any* improvement initiative in *any* business.

One way to focus the discussion around project value is to seek the answers to some key questions. Check these questions out.

Q1. Why is this opportunity worth taking on?

Q2. Why is it worth taking on *now*?

Q3. How does this opportunity fit with the strategic objectives of the business?

Q4. What projects or activities have equal or higher priority than this?

Q5. What are the potential financial benefits of this opportunity?

Q6. What are the risks for us if we do not undertake this opportunity?

Where questions 1 to 3 cannot be answered, you have to question why you would even consider this an opportunity in the first place.

Screening For Process Improvement Opportunities

Some opportunities for improvement will be simple projects requiring a straight forward problem solving / idea generation or solution design approach. For example the opportunity to 'access a company's online platform via smart-phone' will require the design and development of some sort of phone application. It's clearly a business improvement (or growth) idea that necessitates the use of both software development and project management skills.

By contrast, some opportunities will guide focus towards improving an existing process. For example the opportunity to 'reduce the number of dry solder defects' being experienced for an electronic item requires a team to work on improving the 'soldering process' in some way. In this case we have a 'process improvement' opportunity.

Let's focus on this concept of process improvement for a while.

Process Improvement

While there are many processes in an organisation, there is only a small number of types of processes that exist.

Some processes are highly standardised whilst others are not, some occur with high frequency whilst others do not. If we blend these two characteristics into a matrix and provide examples of the various forms of process, we get this.

	Low Frequency	High Frequency
High Standardisation	Flying a plane Racing a formula one car Conducting a training course	Manufacturing standard components in a production line Making a Cafe Latte in a roadside snack bar Fitting replacement tyres for motor vehicles
Low Standardisation	Painting a piece of artwork Writing a score of music Making a movie Constructing a custom designed building	Equipment breakdown repairs Safe work process (particularly evident in the mining industry)

Process Types

Is it a Lean Six Sigma Project or not?

The *project* sequences of Lean Six Sigma (known widely as DMAIC) and Design for Six Sigma (known most commonly as DMADV) both apply to processes that are **repetitive** in nature; that is the cycle occurs frequently *and* it the process is executed in a standardised sequence.

The suite of tools from Lean Six Sigma (in a project context) are used when working on and improving an *existing* process. By contrast, the process *design* tools are intended for developing processes that do not yet exist.

So at a basic level, any improvement opportunity that is based on ...

a. an EXISTING process,

b. that is used (or cycled) FREQUENTLY,

c. in a a highly STANDARDISED way ...

... is suitable as a good fit Lean Six Sigma project.

Having said that, let's recognise that the tools of Lean and Six Sigma can be used to help with work for *any* improvement project. For example, a team working on a one-off process may find it useful to use the process mapping tools or data collection planning tools from the suite of tools.

Alternatives to Lean Six Sigma

Any number of potential projects will probably not fit the 'Lean Six Sigma Project' screen. Those improvement ideas are still evaluated and prioritised according to the value they bring to the business.

Prioritise Opportunities

Weighted Criteria Rating is used by many companies throughout the world to prioritise improvement projects. The term *weighted* criteria alludes to the idea that some criterion are more important than others and are weighted accordingly. These criteria can be considered as those qualities that are desirable in a project; these are the 'should have' criteria.

Criteria

Criteria is often selected through discussion with members of the business leadership team. The list of criteria answers the question - 'What qualities or attributes do we want our projects to have for the initiative to contribute to the achievement of strategic business goals?'

The criteria shown in the example below are based on the following principles.

- The greater the **accessibility of quality data**, the greater the opportunity for success

- The greater the **financial benefit**, the more value the opportunity potentially brings to the business

- The more amenable the opportunity is to **effective implementation** the more attractive the project

- The faster a project can be completed, the **earlier benefits** will be experienced and the greater the chance of success

- The greater the **contribution to business objectives**, the higher the level of value offered to stakeholders

The following diagram shows an example of project prioritisation using weighted criteria linked to the principles listed above.

	SELECTION CRITERIA					
	Access to Data	Financial Return	Change Effort Expected	Expected Time to Complete	Impact on Business Objectives	
Weighting	2	4	3	3	5	
IDEA	5 Excellent 3 Average 1 Poor	5 High 3 Med 1 Low	5 Easy 3 Moderate 1 Hard	5 < 8 wks 3 8 - 16 wks 1 > 16 wks	5 High 3 Med 1 Low	**RATING** **(Max 85)**
Project A	4	5	5	5	5	83
Project B	3	5	3	3	3	59
Project C	2	5	1	1	5	55

Weighted Criteria Rating

Weightings

Weightings are allocated to the criteria by virtue of how *important* each one is to the business.

One is usually selected as the most important criteria and allocated the maximum weighting, with the others being allocated according to the priority given by the team. In the example shown, 'Impact on Business Objectives' has received the maximum rating of '5' as the most important criteria.

Overall Ratings

The overall rating given to each project is calculated by multiplying the rating given against each criteria, by the respective weighting for each criteria. These values are then added together to give the overall rating value.

For example, Project B is given a rating of 4 for the criteria 'Quality of Data'. This is multiplied by the weighting value of 2 to give its weighted rating.

This process is repeated for each of the criterion, and the weighted values are then added up to give the final rating of 83 out of a possible 85. This project is of a higher priority than Project D which received a lower overall rating of 59, and Project F which received the lowest overall rating of 55.

Rating Against The 'Data' Criteria

A Lean Six Sigma project team *must* have access to data. It's an essential requirement for *any* project where cause and effect relationships is determined by the historical behaviour of certain variables. Six Sigma is particularly focused on quantitative data.

The process consists of three steps:

Step 1 - Determine the accessibility of data: classify it as as either easy or hard to access.

Step 2 - Determine the quality of data: classify it as either high or low quality.

Step 3 - Select the appropriate quadrant that corresponds to these classifications and use the rating indicated.

For example, a project with easily accessible data but low quality would be given a rating of 3. A project with easily accessible data of high quality would be given a rating of 5.

The following matrix may prove useful in allocating a rating against 'Data' criteria when prioritising improvement projects.

	Low Quality	High Quality
Easy to Access	3	5
Difficult to Access	1	3

Rating Quality of Data

It may be the case that some potential projects have limited data availability. This may be more a measurement problem than a Lean Six Sigma fit problem. With this though in mind, any project may be reassessed at any time subsequent to the undertaking of data collection activities for the particular process.

By recognising this aspect of project selection, coordinators should be able to capture all worthwhile projects as time progresses.

Rating Against The 'Impact On Business Objectives' Criteria

Contribution and benefits can be rated according to a scale ranging from insignificant to significant. The table shown offers a guide to allocating relevant ratings for inclusion in the 'Weighted Criteria Rating' tool.

Rating	Descriptor	Contribution to Business Objectives	Financial Benefits (1st Year)
1	Insignificant	Insignificant impact on key performance metrics	< $50K
2	Minor	Small impact on key performance metrics	$50K to $250K
3	Moderate	Moderate impact on key performance metrics	$250K to $500K
4	Major	Major impact on key performance metrics	$500K to $1M
5	Significant	Significant impact on key performance metrics	> $1M

Rating Impact on Business Objectives

Rating Against The 'Change Effort' Criteria

The degree of effort associated with any change will be driven by the degree of resistance to the change that is experienced. Accordingly, effort can be rated according to a scale ranging from easy to hard, based on expected resistance.

Rating	Descriptor	Contribution to Business Objectives
1	Hard	Significant widespread resistance to implementation of a solution may be experienced.
2	Moderately Hard	Major resistance to implementation of a solution from a small group may be experienced.
3	Moderate	Some resistance may be experienced but it is unlikely that this would prevent successful implementation of a solution.
4	Moderately Easy	Some resistance may be experienced but would have no impact on solution implementation.
5	Easy	There would be widespread support for implementation of a solution and no resistance would be experienced.

Rating Change Effort

In conclusion, project selection forms an important element of the Business Improvement Operating System. Without an effective selection process, challenges will be experienced with respect to:

1. Rapidly generating returns to the business;

2. Sustaining focus on Business Improvement as a key growth strategy; and

3. Sustainability of a formal Business Improvement initiative over the long term.

When an effective selection process is established, benefits will be experienced with respect to:

1. The cyclic rate of project work;

2. The development of quality Business Improvement practitioners; and

3. Growth in organisation value.

Allocate Projects Wisely

First Time Lean Six Sigma Black Belt / Green Belt

The first project for a Black Belt of Green Belt in training can be quite daunting. Even though they may be receiving 'just in time' training, they have been given quite a large tool kit to work with.

This time is critical in the development of competent project team leaders in the shortest period of time; therefore projects for first time Lean Six Sigma Black Belts or Green Belts will ideally meet the following criteria:

- A highly REPETITIVE process.

- Quality DATA is available, or if not available now can be easily obtained.

- Provides opportunities to apply as many TOOLS as possible.

- Be EXECUTABLE in a time frame of no longer than 4 to 6 weeks.

- Requires the participation of a PROJECT TEAM.

- A high probability of SUCCESS.

Keep these in mind when you choose and allocate your Lean Six Sigma projects. Let's set the next generation of practitioners up for success right from the start.

Chapter 9 - Selling and Managing Projects

All Projects Involve Selling

One idea often not considered at the project level of business improvement is the need to sell. When I say 'sell', I'm referring to the process of generating *buy-in to change* during the course of the project.

Let's acknowledge this ... improvement is simply a code word for change. And it stands to reason that at some point in time during an improvement project, it *will be* necessary to work with people in order to have them change their behaviour.

The Greatest Challenge

Changing processes is not the challenge; that's easy.

I have absolutely no doubts that the greatest challenge for *any* business leader is changing people. And here's the reality ... it's not getting any easier. The more educated people are, the greater their focus on lifestyle, and the more they see opportunities that exist on a global front; the greater the requirement for a leader to use the tools of influence and persuasion.

Traditional command and control styles are not the singular focus of the most effective leaders today. In my experience, the singular focus on that style of leadership, or any style for that matter, will always be limited in its affect. The most effective leaders now realise they have to not only command, but *also* be able to influence the thinking and emotions of an audience in order to get them to *willingly* do something.

This is true for modern day Master Black Belts as well. The reason why our MBB program is so popular today is because we've recognised that a MBB is no longer just a statistically better trained Black Belt. The focus of

MBB development must now be on developing their skills of influence and massively increasing their use of persuasion techniques.

You can read more about this topic in my blog - How Master Black Belts are in danger of becoming irrelevant.

So how does sales and change integrate *into* the normal project sequence?

As an experienced improvement practitioner, I'm guessing you already know quite a bit about this. Let me add to what you know with a couple of ideas.

Selling And Change Is Part Of The Sequence

The diagram below shows a generic sequence for a project designed to develop and implement solutions. The points along that sequence where change and selling is required are indicated by the red marks.

Selling and Getting Buy-in In A Project

Notice that as a general rule, getting buy-in and creating behaviour change is necessary at certain points:

1. The project itself needs to be sold to those who will provide resources, without their buy-in it will be a struggle

2. Not only do we develop a technical plan for changing the process or thing in question, we also need a plan for the soft side [or people side] of rolling out the change

3. Sometimes we will be required to *sell the plan* to key stakeholders *before* we roll it out

4. And finally ... we have to lock in any changes requiring human involvement

While this is not a book specifically teaching how to sell or create permanent change, let's at least talk about the creation of a business case for the project.

Creating The Business Case

We said this in the previous section - *all* improvement projects undertaken must add *value* to the business in some way.

What's more, the value it brings is the cornerstone for *selling* the project to those who need to support it most ... the leaders of the business. If you want buy-in and support then be prepared to answer these questions.

Q1. Why is this opportunity worth taking on?

Q2. Why is it worth taking on *now*?

Q3. How does this opportunity fit with the strategic objectives of the business?

Q4. What projects or activities have equal or higher priority than this?

Q5. What are the potential financial benefits of this opportunity?

Q6. What are the risks [or downside] for us if we do not undertake this opportunity?

All Projects Must Be Managed

Project Start Up

Before a team is brought together to begin the project, some work associated with starting the project must be completed. In fact this work needs to be commenced *before* a team is even selected.

The questions that specifically need answering at this point in time include:

Q1. What is the real problem or opportunity we are going to work on?

Q2. Who should comprise the members of the team?

Q3. What is the scope of the project .... what's in and what's out?

Q4. What are the constraints or limitations that will impact access to resources as well as the decisions of the team in choosing solutions?

Q5. What is the level of improvement we are going to seek to achieve?

Q6. What is the general schedule of activities the team will engage in to complete this project?

At the end of the Project Start Up phase, the project team leader, process owner and champion should be able to produce:

1. A Business Case (if not previously developed); and

2. A Project Charter.

In my opinion, the responsibility for preparing these rests with the Project Champion, not the team.

Final Notes For Sponsors And Process Owners

Are you a project champion or a process owner connected with some project?

If you are then definitely keep these tips in mind.

One of the most critical roles during execution of a Lean Six Sigma project, or *any* project for that matter, is that of a project champion. Without the backing of a line manager who champions the project, even the best project team leaders will find it difficult to function. In my experience, a project champion can have a *dramatic* effect on the success of *any* improvement project.

Process Owners can also have a tremendous impact on project progress. They really are the true sponsors of the project work. Their role in providing resources and making sure sustained changes take place is vital to long-term success.

Leading Behaviours

Some of the leading behaviours worth modeling are these.

Actually ... let me be more definitive about this. You MUST model these behaviours.

(1) Build an Operating Agreement Up Front

At the commencement of the project, establish a *clear* agreement with the team leader on:

(a) What you will do *for the team leader* (ask the team leader what they expect of you and then outline details of what the team leader can expect of you);

(b) What you *expect of the team leader* (ask the team leader what they will do for you and then outline details of what you expect the team leader will do); and finally

(c) The level of decision making the team can make *without* your approval (this requires the clarification of constraints or limitations to decision making).

The details of these agreements should be captured in writing and shared with the team leader. Work in this area avoids the pain of conflict, procrastination and unnecessary surprises.

(2) Avoid Micro Managing

Don't get caught up in the details of the project or the content. Leave it alone.

Your role is to provide all of the support your project team leader requires to accelerate the project to a successful conclusion ... that's it.

Your efforts should focus on ensuring effective team dynamics, project progress, elimination of barriers, and helping to influence change.

Master the macro issues! Do this and the team will follow you anywhere.

(3) Scope Down

Almost *every* project that I have ever reviewed, and the number is in the 1000's, suffered from too large a scope during the start up and early phases. Not only is the team expected to fix the process, it's a case of 'while you're there' you might as well fix the rest of the business. If you want to kill momentum in a team, load them up with an overwhelming project that seems to be endless.

I've also observed countless project team leaders exhibit tremendous frustration when business leaders increase the scope of their projects. You know the term ...'scope creep'. What's interesting is that those team leaders tend to avoid entering into debate about the issue for they fear conflict will result. So ... the matter never gets resolves. The project just struggles.

In fact, project champions and process owners are often not even aware that scope is an issue until the project time frame goes way beyond original expectations.

Do yourself and the team a favour ... scope the project down to a manageable size chunk that the *team* believes is reasonable and allows the team to focus their efforts in a meaningful way.

(4) Keep the Project On Your Agenda

Give the team leader and the project your attention. That means taking an active interest in meetings and project progress.

This goes way beyond calling the team leader to your office, or giving the team leader free access to you when he or she needs to talk to you. You have to *do* something; remember commitment is demonstrated through action.

- Be proactive in asking the team leader and team members about the project.

- Schedule time to sit in on portions of some project team meetings, but avoid exerting your influence on those meetings when you do attend.

- Talk about the project to your other employees.

(5) Hold The Team Leader Accountable

At the commencement of the project you'll have established agreements about time frames for completion of work. You *must* hold the team leader accountable for those agreed schedules. To do so means asking questions about progress and changes to schedules before deadlines arrive – your active interest and curiosity will keep the team leader focused. Questions like these are useful:

Q. Are we on track with the project?

Q. What's impacting progress that I can help with?

Q. What can I do to help you get back on track?

(6) Eliminate Barriers To Progress

Your job is to keep the team from being distracted by outside demands, and you must fight those battles that are beyond the influence of the team.

Oh ... and by the way ... you must stand by the team when they make mistakes – this is the process of learning and the key to creating a culture of improvement.

Let me leave you with this thought ...

Choose to be a great project champion or process owner and model great leadership behaviour!

_____

Conclusion

Okay ... that's it.

I won't ramble on here. What I will do is simply remind you of the key idea here - that project identification and selection is one of the most important elements for driving success with business improvement in *any* organisation.

If I were to leave you with a piece of advice, it would be this.

1. Take the time to explore the *different* methods of improvement idea generation, its the only way to develop broad experience

2. Be scientific in your approach and *avoid* choosing projects simply because they are somebody's 'pet project'

3. Ask the tough questions about the business case for projects, any business improvement initiative that does not deliver against business objectives *will* eventually be eliminated

4. *Never* be afraid to drop a project, even midway through completion, if it is not going to bring value to the organisation

I wish you good fortune, see you in my next book.

George Lee Sye

About the Author

George Lee Sye was born in 1959, he has found his niche as an author, influence and persuasion educator, and business improvement trainer and coach.

George founded Soarent Vision Pty Ltd in 2000 and has continually run that company as Managing Director.

He founded his first Professional Learning Hub in 2016, and then converted this into what is now the 9 Skills Factory professional development platform. He is the site's lead trainer and this is where he delivers the bulk of the business improvement (lean six sigma and leadership) education to the world.

George launched his podcast The George Experiment in 2018.

His breadth and depth of knowledge is drawn from a diverse range of experiences and life-long commitment to self education - from tradesman - to counter terrorism expert - to protecting the President of the United States of America; from working in horse stables - to Training Manager - to Hospital Administrator - to Company Owner.

Tens of thousands of people have personally experienced his philosophies in formal training courses and seminars, and connected with his incredible enthusiasm and energy for life through his work.

Since 2002 he has written 17 books, most of which are now distributed on Amazon and on iTunes in digital form.

George is also an avid motorcycle enthusiast with the ultimate part time job as an on track ride coach with the California Superbike School.

Photo of the author riding at Phillip Island GP Circuit is courtesy of SD Pics Photography

For more information about George and his work, visit his websites:

www.georgeleesye.com

www.9skillsfactory.com

www.thegeorgeexperiment.com

Lightning Source UK Ltd.
Milton Keynes UK
UKHW020639120422
401447UK00010B/1917